BLACK TRAILBLAZERS IN SPORTS

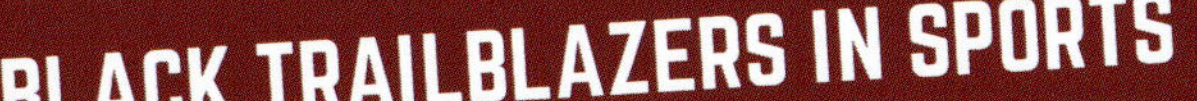

JACKIE ROBINSON

by David Lee Morgan Jr.

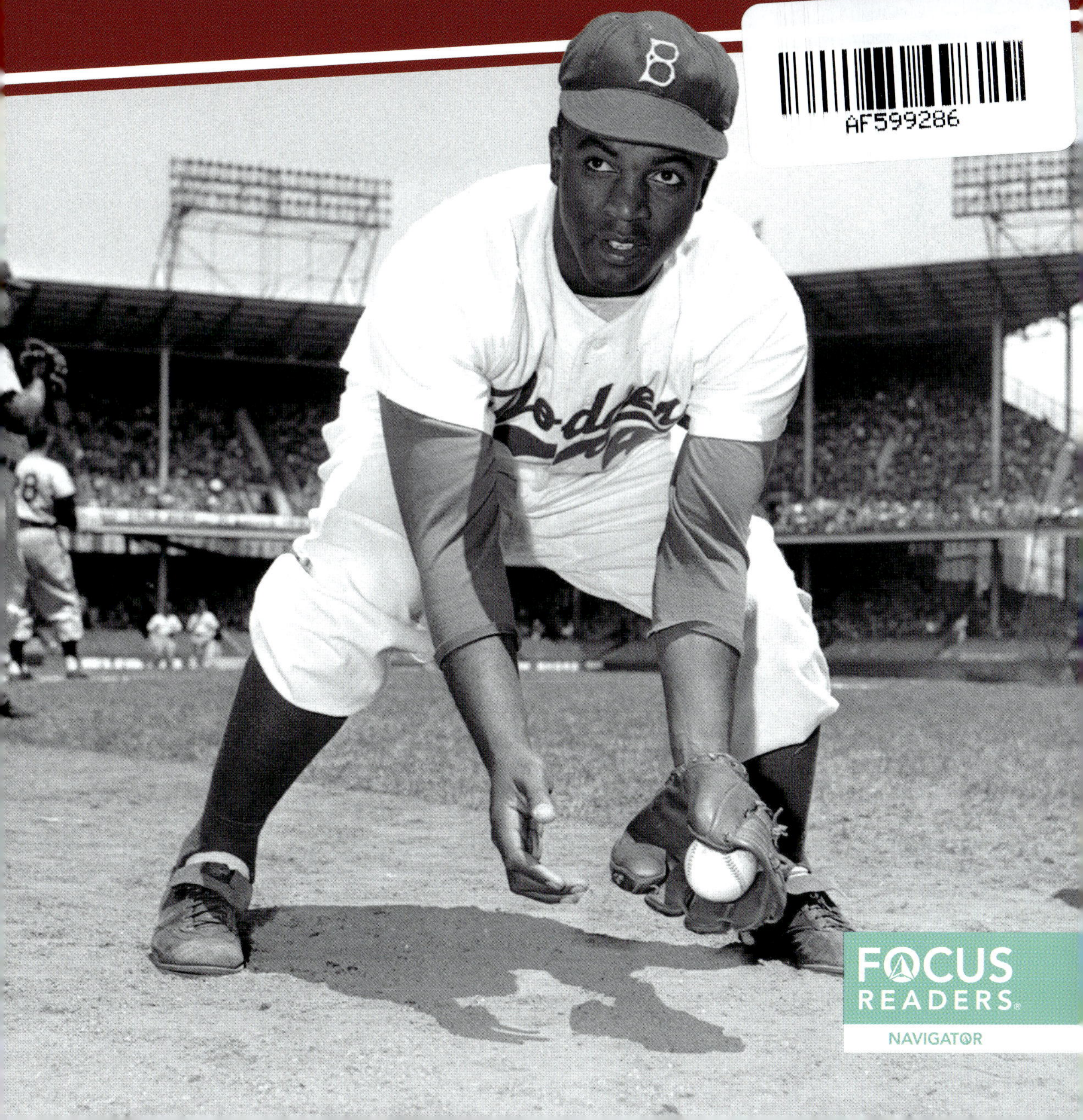

FOCUS READERS

NAVIGATOR

WWW.FOCUSREADERS.COM

Focus Readers is distributed by North Star Editions:
sales@northstareditions.com | 888-417-0195

Produced for Focus Readers by Red Line Editorial.

Photographs ©: AP Images, cover, 1, 14, 16–17; John Lent/AP Images, 4–5, 7; Bettmann/Getty Images, 8, 13, 18, 21, 22–23, 25; Hulton Archive/Getty Images, 10–11; Thos Robinson/Getty Images for Jackie Robinson Foundation/Getty Images Entertainment/Getty Images, 27; Red Line Editorial, 29

Library of Congress Cataloging-in-Publication Data
Names: Morgan, David Lee, author.
Title: Jackie Robinson / by David Lee Morgan, Jr.
Description: Mendota Heights, MN: Focus Readers, [2025] | Series: Black trailblazers in sports | Includes bibliographical references and index. | Audience: Grades 4-6
Identifiers: LCCN 2023053992 (print) | LCCN 2023053993 (ebook) | ISBN 9798889982111 (hardcover) | ISBN 9798889982678 (paperback) | ISBN 9798889983743 (pdf) | ISBN 9798889983231 (ebook)
Subjects: LCSH: Robinson, Jackie, 1919-1972--Juvenile literature. | Infielders (Baseball)--United States--Biography--Juvenile literature. | African American baseball players--Georgia--Biography--Juvenile literature. | Kansas City Monarchs (Baseball team)--Juvenile literature. | Brooklyn Dodgers (Baseball team)--Juvenile literature. | Rookie of the Year Award (Baseball)--Juvenile literature. | African American civil rights workers--Georgia--Biography--Juvenile literature. | National Association for the Advancement of Colored People--Juvenile literature. | Freedom National Bank (New York, N.Y.)--Juvenile literature. | Jackie Robinson Foundation--Juvenile literature.
Classification: LCC GV865.R6 M67 2025 (print) | LCC GV865.R6 (ebook) | DDC 796.357092 [B]--dc23/eng/20231213
LC record available at https://lccn.loc.gov/2023053992
LC ebook record available at https://lccn.loc.gov/2023053993

Printed in the United States of America
Mankato, MN
082024

ABOUT THE AUTHOR

David Lee Morgan Jr. is the author of 11 books, including *LeBron James: The Rise of a Star* and *Breaking Through the Lines: The Marion Motley Story*. Morgan was a longtime sportswriter with the *Akron Beacon Journal* and is now a high school English teacher and public speaker.

TABLE OF CONTENTS

Montreal

CHAPTER 1

A HANDSHAKE FOR THE CENTURY

Jackie Robinson stepped up to the plate for his second at-bat. It was Opening Day of the 1946 baseball season. Robinson was making his **debut** with the Montreal Royals. The Royals were one of the Brooklyn Dodgers' minor league teams. At the time, Robinson was the only Black player in the minor

Jackie Robinson (right) poses with the Montreal Royals manager before Opening Day in 1946.

leagues. There were no Black players in Major League Baseball (MLB) either.

A crowd of 52,000 fans filled Roosevelt Stadium in New Jersey. The Royals were on the road facing the Jersey City Giants. Robinson's wife, Rachel, was in the crowd. She felt nervous for her husband. She wanted him to have a good game. Some fans in Montreal had embraced Robinson. But other fans called him **racist** names. They believed Black players didn't belong on the same field as white players.

Robinson was determined to prove he belonged. In his second at-bat, he hit a home run with two runners on base. The runners crossed home plate as Robinson

Robinson slides into third base during the 1946 Opening Day game.

rounded the bases. But they didn't wait to congratulate Robinson for the home run. Instead, they went straight into the dugout. Even so, Robinson crossed home plate with a huge smile on his face.

Robinson shakes teammate George Shuba's hand after a home run on Opening Day.

The first person to greet Robinson was his teammate George Shuba. He was the next batter for the Royals. Shuba waited for Robinson at the plate. He reached out his hand to congratulate Robinson on his home run.

The handshake was a historic moment in sports. It showed a white man accepting his Black teammate when others didn't. A photographer captured the moment. The photo became known as *A Handshake for the Century*. It was the first picture of Black and white players congratulating each other on the baseball field.

The Royals easily won the game 14–1. Robinson recorded four hits and four runs batted in (RBIs). However, the star second baseman wasn't in the minor leagues for long. The following year, Robinson made even more history. This time, it was on a much bigger stage.

CHAPTER 2

A LEGEND IS BORN

Jack Roosevelt Robinson was born in Cairo, Georgia, in 1919. He was the youngest of five children. His father left the family in 1920. Jackie's mother decided to move with her kids to Pasadena, California.

The Robinsons were poor. They were not welcomed by the white families who

A young Jackie Robinson poses for a picture in 1925.

lived nearby. Even so, Jackie's mother worked hard to make money. She cleaned and cooked for wealthy white families.

Jackie's athletic ability was clear by high school. He took part in track, football, basketball, baseball, and tennis. Jackie dealt with racism even though he was a star athlete. Many white people did

MACK ROBINSON

Jackie Robinson's older brother Mack was a great track athlete. He competed in the 1936 Olympic Games in Berlin. He won the silver medal in the 200-meter race. He finished just 0.4 seconds behind the gold medal winner, Jesse Owens. Owens was one of the greatest athletes in Olympic history.

Robinson carries the ball during a 1939 game with the University of California, Los Angeles.

not want to see him succeed. Some of them were his teammates.

Robinson continued competing. After high school, he went to a local college for a year. Then he started attending the University of California, Los Angeles (UCLA). He played football, basketball,

Robinson was an All-Star during his one year with the Kansas City Monarchs.

and baseball, and he ran track. He became the first UCLA athlete to earn **varsity** letters in four sports.

World War II (1939–1945) interrupted Robinson's post-college career. He served in the US military for three years. After the war, he went right back to sports. In 1945, Robinson signed a baseball contract with the Kansas City Monarchs. The Monarchs were in the **Negro leagues**.

MLB teams soon noticed Robinson. Branch Rickey, a white man, was looking for Black players to sign. He was the president and general manager of the Brooklyn Dodgers.

Rickey saw Robinson's talent. So, in late 1945, he signed Robinson to the Dodgers' minor league team. Robinson excelled with the Montreal Royals. He led the team to the league championship. It was clear that he was ready for the next level.

Dodgers
Phillies

CHAPTER 3

BREAKING BARRIERS

Jackie Robinson played his first MLB game on April 15, 1947. He became the first Black player in MLB's modern era. Robinson faced extreme racism while playing in MLB. During games, people yelled racist **slurs** at him. Some people even made death threats against him. Branch Rickey told Robinson to ignore

The racism Robinson faced in 1947 in Pennsylvania was extreme. The Phillies manager took a photo with him to try to stop it.

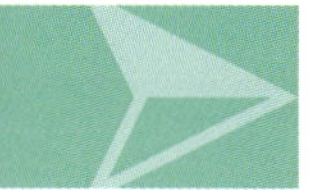

Robinson stole home 19 times during his career with the Brooklyn Dodgers.

these people. He said to focus on playing instead.

It was hard for Robinson, but he knew he had a big responsibility. He wanted to set an example for other Black players to follow. So, he learned to stay calm and hold back his anger.

Robinson's efforts paid off. He helped the Dodgers reach the World Series that season. They ended up losing to the New York Yankees. But Robinson had a great year. He finished the regular season with a .297 batting average. Robinson played so well he won the Rookie of the Year Award.

That was just the beginning for Robinson. In 1949, he dominated baseball. Robinson led the league in both hitting and steals. He batted a career-high .342. And he stole 37 bases. Robinson also racked up 124 RBIs. That was a career best for him. His performance earned him the NL Most

Valuable Player (MVP) Award. He became the first Black player to win the award.

Robinson made his first All-Star team in 1949, too. He went on to make the team every year through 1954. He also led Brooklyn back to the World Series in 1949, 1952, and 1953. Each time, the

NO. 42

Over the years, MLB has honored Robinson in many ways. In 1997, MLB retired Robinson's No. 42. That means no new player in the league can wear his number. And in 2004, the league made April 15 Jackie Robinson Day. On that day, all players, coaches, managers, and umpires wear No. 42 in his honor.

The Dodgers rush the field to celebrate after winning the 1955 World Series.

Dodgers faced the Yankees. But each time, the Yankees came out on top.

Robinson and the Dodgers got another rematch with their rival in 1955. This time, Brooklyn won in a seven-game series. Robinson was a World Series champion!

42

CHAPTER 4

LIFE AFTER BASEBALL

Jackie Robinson's last season in the major leagues was in 1956. The Dodgers made it back to the World Series that year. But they fell to the Yankees once again. In December, Robinson was traded to the New York Giants. However, he decided to leave baseball instead. He was 37 years old. Robinson wanted to

The Dodgers reached the World Series six times during Robinson's 10 years with the team.

begin a new life outside the sport. He wanted to spend more time with his wife and their three children.

Robinson worked a variety of jobs. First, he became the vice president at a coffee company and restaurant. Robinson also worked as a TV announcer. He wrote articles for newspapers and magazines, too.

Robinson also worked for Black Americans' **civil rights**. He helped groups such as the National Association for the Advancement of Colored People (NAACP). He even became friends with civil rights leader Dr. Martin Luther King Jr.

Robinson joins a protest in 1963 about racist hiring practices in New York.

Robinson helped poor Black people in other ways. In 1964, he helped create the Freedom National Bank. This bank was in Harlem in New York City. Many low-income Black people lived there. The bank helped with finances for these communities. And in 1970, Robinson started the Jackie Robinson Construction Company. He wanted to provide housing for poor people.

Over the years, Robinson's health declined. He died on October 24, 1972, of heart disease and diabetes. He was only 53. However, his family kept

BLACK MLB MANAGERS

After retiring, Jackie Robinson always wanted to see a Black manager in MLB. He spoke out about it, too. Two years after Robinson died, Cleveland named Frank Robinson manager. He became the first Black manager in MLB history. Frank and Jackie weren't related. But Frank knew who to thank. It was Jackie.

In 2017, Robinson's family celebrated the groundbreaking of the Jackie Robinson Museum in New York City.

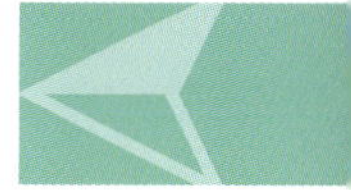

Robinson's **legacy** alive. They started the Jackie Robinson Foundation in 1973. This group gives **scholarships** to students of color who want to attend college.

JACKIE ROBINSON

- **Height:** 5 feet 11 inches (180 cm)
- **Weight:** 195 pounds (88 kg)
- **Born:** January 31, 1919
- **Died:** October 24, 1972
- **Birthplace:** Cairo, Georgia
- **High school:** John Muir Technical High School (Pasadena, California)
- **Colleges:** Pasadena City College; University of California, Los Angeles
- **Negro leagues team:** Kansas City Monarchs (1945)
- **Minor league team:** Montreal Royals (1946)
- **MLB team:** Brooklyn Dodgers (1947–56)
- **Major achievements:** NL Rookie of the Year (1947); NL MVP (1949); NL Batting Title (1949); MLB All-Star (1949–54); World Series champion (1955); Baseball Hall of Fame (1962)

Montreal
Brooklyn
Pasadena
Kansas City
Los Angeles
Cairo

FOCUS ON
JACKIE ROBINSON

Write your answers on a separate sheet of paper.

1. Write a paragraph explaining the main ideas of Chapter 3.
2. Jackie Robinson experienced racism throughout his athletic career. Why do you think he continued playing?
3. Where was Robinson born?
   - **A.** Los Angeles, California
   - **B.** Cairo, Georgia
   - **C.** Brooklyn, New York
4. How does the Jackie Robinson Foundation help keep Robinson's legacy alive?
   - **A.** The foundation helps only members of Robinson's family.
   - **B.** The foundation teaches people how to play baseball like Robinson.
   - **C.** Students learn about Robinson when they receive educational support.

Answer key on page 32.

GLOSSARY

civil rights
Rights that protect people's freedom and equality.

debut
First appearance.

legacy
The things a person becomes known for.

Negro leagues
Professional baseball leagues made up of Black players who weren't allowed to play in the all-white leagues.

racist
Having to do with hatred or mistreatment of people because of their skin color or ethnicity.

scholarships
Money given to students to pay for education expenses.

slurs
Terms that are insulting and hurtful.

varsity
The top team representing a high school or college in a sport or competition.

TO LEARN MORE

BOOKS

Allen, John. *Important Black Americans in Sports*. San Diego: ReferencePoint Press, 2023.

Hoena, Blake. *Jackie Robinson: Athletes Who Made a Difference*. Minneapolis: Lerner Publications, 2020.

Williams, Yohuru, and Michael G. Long. *Call Him Jack: The Story of Jackie Robinson, Black Freedom Fighter*. New York: Farrar Straus Giroux, 2022.

NOTE TO EDUCATORS

Visit **www.focusreaders.com** to find lesson plans, activities, links, and other resources related to this title.

INDEX

Answer Key: 1. Answers will vary; **2.** Answers will vary; **3.** B; **4.** C